SWOOP AND SOAR

By Deborah Lee Rose and Jane Veltkamp

PERSNICKETY PRESS

Designed by Brian Scott Sockin

ISBN: 978-1-943978-56-4

Printed in USA

10 9 8 7 6 5 4 3 2 1

Produced by **Persnickety Press**
An imprint of WunderMill, inc.
321 Glen Echo Lane, Suite C
Cary, NC 27518

www.WunderMillBooks.com

For Janie and Don Veltkamp and all who rescue, and for Judy, who showed me where ospreys swoop and soar—DLR

For wildlife biologists Wayne Melquist, who inspired my osprey work, and Jack Payne, who went above and beyond to help rescue these two ospreys—JV

The names of the osprey chicks in this story—Swoop and Soar— were inspired by birds in flight. We chose these names so our readers will always remember that these real ospreys are wild creatures, and Janie's work was to return them to the wild.

SWOOP AND SOAR

HOW SCIENCE RESCUED TWO OSPREY ORPHANS AND FOUND THEM A NEW FAMILY IN THE WILD

By Deborah Lee Rose and Jane Veltkamp

PERSNICKETY PRESS

High above the dark blue water, a sharp-beaked osprey hovered in the morning sky. He had been hunting since first light to catch food for his hungry chicks. Suddenly his yellow eyes saw something glimmer in the waves far below.

In an instant, the osprey plunged downward with his talons wide open in front of him. He crashed through the shallow waves feet first and disappeared!

The osprey broke back up through the surface, a shimmering fish clamped in his talons. With powerful beats of his wings, the osprey lifted himself out of the water and into the air.

As he flew, he shook his whole body to fling any water off his feathers. Then the osprey flipped the fish in his talons, so it faced the same direction he was flying.

Now the osprey could move faster through the air to reach his forest nest and chicks.

Just as the osprey neared land, a bald eagle started chasing him. The osprey swerved to the left and right trying to escape, but the eagle was bigger and stronger. Unclenching his talons, the osprey dropped the fish he had worked so hard to catch. The eagle snatched the fish in midair.

The osprey was very hungry, and he still had to feed his family. Again he headed out over the water. While the osprey hunted, his chicks slept in a giant nest of sticks.

At the top of the tallest tree, no raccoons or rattlesnakes could harm them. The baby birds were safe, nestled under their mother's body. The mother osprey's loud call woke the sister and brother. Their father had brought a fish! The chicks started chirping, begging for food.

With quick, strong twists of her head,
their mother used her beak to rip off pieces of fish.
Then gently, she held the bites to her chicks' open mouths.

After the babies gulped their food, the mother osprey spread
her wings like an umbrella. She would shade her nestlings all
afternoon from the Sun's burning rays.

By late afternoon, the weather had changed. Fast-moving storm clouds covered the Sun. All the sailboats and fishing boats had come back into the harbor near the forest.

Lightning bolts began to split the sky. Booms of thunder shook the forest canopy. Heavy rain poured down on the nest, while the wind swayed the tree branches wildly from side to side. The wind's force grew stronger, pushing the tree to a steeper and steeper slant.

As the roots pulled out of the rain-soaked soil, the whole tree crashed down. The crash threw the baby birds into the air, but they didn't know how to fly. They fell hard on the forest floor, near their shattered nest. With only thin, soft feathers covering their bodies, the brother and sister huddled together shivering in the darkness.

The next morning, a rainbow gleamed over the water.

In the forest a woodpecker hammered and songbirds trilled, as if the storm had never happened. But where the tree had stood, the osprey parents flew in circles looking and calling for their lost chicks.

A wildlife biologist named Jack lived near the forest. Before the storm, he had watched through his binoculars as the father osprey brought fish to the nest. Now Jack saw the tree and the nest were gone.

Jack knew if the chicks were still alive, their parents couldn't take care of them on the ground. The mother and father would leave to build a new nest, and hatch new eggs.

Jack went searching. He found the baby birds under a broken branch. They were cold and weak. He wrapped them in a towel and took them to a wildlife center. There, the rescue staff put them right into an incubator to keep warm.

The sister and brother were orphans now. Even with special care, they might never go back to the forest.

News of the orphans travelled fast. When a raptor biologist named Janie heard about them, she knew what she had to do. Janie had rescued many ospreys. She would find the orphans a new nest with new osprey parents.

Before the storm, Janie had been watching an osprey nest on a low platform over a fishing dock. Through her magnifying scope, she had seen young chicks in the nest.

Now the chicks were gone from the nest over the dock. Janie realized the storm had blown them into the waves. The baby birds had not survived, but she saw their parents still bringing fish to the empty nest.

Janie knew that without chicks to feed, the mother and father would give up the dock nest in as soon as three days. She had to get the orphans into the nest before the osprey parents flew away and didn't come back.

Janie took over the chicks' care day and night. She called them Swoop and Soar. They were so young, their orange eyes couldn't see that humans were feeding them. Every four hours, Janie and her husband Don held bits of fish to the chicks' beaks.

With plenty of food, Swoop and Soar began holding their heads up and moving their wings. Janie could see they were strong enough to go back into the wild.

The next morning when the osprey parents went hunting, Janie climbed a ladder to the dock nest. Don handed Swoop and Soar up to her. Carefully, she set the brother and sister in the soft grass lining the nest.

After Janie climbed down, she and Don moved to the far side of a wide road to watch the nest. People from the nearby town gathered with them, hoping—would the osprey parents adopt the orphans as their own chicks?

Through her scope, Janie could see Swoop and Soar in the nest. The father brought them a fish, but the mother didn't come to feed them. Two hours went by as the Sun blazed down. The mother landed on a nearby pole, but flew off right away.

Janie was worried. Swoop and Soar were panting, puffing out hot air to try and cool their bodies. If the mother osprey didn't come to shade and feed them, Janie's hopes for the chicks to stay in the nest would be crushed.

After almost four hours, the mother flew into the nest! She spread her wings to shade the baby birds as if they were her very own.

From that moment a new family was born.

Once Swoop and Soar were cooled down, the mother tore off bites of fish. She touched the food to her new babies' beaks, and they opened their mouths wide to eat.

The chicks grew so fast, they needed twice as much food as their new parents.

By four weeks, Swoop and Soar could stand and hop around while their mother and father kept constant watch.

The Sun was just setting when their mother spotted a great-horned owl flying overhead. An owl could steal a chick with one pounce. Their mother whistled a high-pitched "Get down!" call. Quickly, the chicks flattened their bodies in the bottom of the nest for camouflage, till the danger was gone.

By six weeks, Swoop and Soar's wings grew as wide as their parents' wings. The chicks stretched and practiced flapping their wings for hours.

f they flapped hard enough, they could lift themselves above the nest. One afternoon, a strong gust of wind carried Swoop past the edge of the nest.

Swoop flapped and flapped in a wobbly loop through the air, then landed so hard in the nest, he bumped Soar over the edge.

Soar's talons grabbed the sticks at the nest's edge, but she was hanging upside down like a bat! She started flapping, then let go with her talons. She fell towards the water, till her wings lifted her up and up, back to her family.

Every day Swoop and Soar flew farther, but catching fish was hard. Sometimes after they dove into the water, they couldn't lift their bodies back into the air. They had to use their wings like oars, to row themselves back to shore.

Once the chicks learned to catch all their food, their parents didn't need to feed them anymore. The mother and father both flew away, this time to begin their migrations.

Soon Swoop and Soar were ready to migrate too. Each on their own now flew to faraway places they had never been.

While they were away, their bodies slowly changed. Their eyes turned from orange to yellow. Their pale-tipped brown feathers molted and sleek, black feathers grew in.

Two years later, Swoop and Soar began their journeys home.

They flew for days without resting. Finally back near the place where they had learned to fly, the brother and sister found mates and began building new nests. By the shallow waters filled with fish, they would start to raise their own chicks in the wild.

A note from raptor biologist Janie Veltkamp

Rescuing ospreys

To put the rescued osprey chicks we call Swoop and Soar back into the wild, I had to know the science of young ospreys' life cycle. The orphans were only 10 days old—and their eyes couldn't see yet—so it was safe for me to feed them, without them becoming imprinted and dependent on humans.

To get the orphans "adopted" was a race against time. I had observed that the parents in the dock nest lost their own chicks in the storm. The parents would fly away within 3 days, so I had to put the orphans in the new nest quickly. "Cross fostering" the chicks into the new nest gave them a second chance in the wild.

My life's work is rescuing and treating ospreys, and other injured and sick raptors, to release them back into the wild. Ospreys are awesome, powerful birds. Caring for them takes special training and experience, including how to stay safe when an osprey that needs help tries to defend itself with its sharp talons or twisting bite. Whether I'm fixing an injured osprey's leg that was cut by fishing line, or handling a healed osprey on short, tethered flights to strengthen its wing muscles, all my work needs permission from state and federal wildlife agencies.

Reintroducing ospreys

Ospreys are known as a "bioindicator" species. We share the air, water and trees with them, and they indicate our own future to us. Years ago, ospreys' future looked very, very bad. Widespread use of the insect-killing chemical DDT endangered ospreys, just as it endangered bald eagles and peregrine falcons. Growing up, I never saw an osprey because their species was so devastated.

Even after the U.S. banned DDT, ospreys desperately needed help to recover their populations. In eastern South Dakota, ospreys had become extinct, and first efforts to reintroduce ospreys there had failed. I was now a raptor biologist—and had helped reintroduce peregrine falcons in Indiana—so I agreed to lead a new osprey project.

Wings Over Water relocated 60 young osprey chicks from Idaho, where there were plenty of ospreys, to eastern South Dakota. As other projects had done to rebuild raptor populations, our team reintroduced the chicks while they were still too young to fly. We raised them in human-built nests, or hacking boxes, on special release towers. While we never showed ourselves to the chicks—so they wouldn't become imprinted on humans—we put food in their nests through large tubes or chutes. We kept watch with video cameras as they grew.

Soon the chicks took their first flights, or fledged. Over many weeks, we observed as they learned to catch all their own fish and moved fully into their new wild territory. Once these reintroduced ospreys began their migrations, they would likely return to eastern South Dakota—where they had learned to fly—and raise many new chicks.

From Wings Over Water, I learned firsthand how far ospreys could migrate. To track the chicks on their early flights, we put leg bands on them and painted bits of color on their wings. Months later, when these ospreys were on their first long migrations, we heard from wildlife watchers in Central America, thousands of miles away. They had photographed one of our ospreys, and contacted us using information from its leg bands. They wanted to know the special meaning of the paint color on the wings.

Protecting ospreys

Like scientists around the world, I observe wild ospreys and other birds to protect their populations and habitats. Watching and protecting help ensure bird species' survival in the face of threats like pollution, habitat destruction, and climate change.

Northern Idaho where I live is home to the largest nesting osprey population west of the Rocky Mountains. In Coeur d'Alene, Idaho, one pair built a nest on top of a lamppost by Lake Coeur d'Alene. Both ospreys and people fish in the lake. People watching the city's osprey nest cam online noticed one chick in the nest had not moved around for a week. City managers called me in for a rescue.

I was transported by bucket truck 80 feet (24 meters) up. I found the chick with one leg completely tangled in plastic fishing line. The line had been attached to a fish the father osprey caught. After the osprey family ate the fish, the line snagged around the chick's leg and tightened. The truck operator and I had to cut away a huge amount of fishing line in the nest. I took the chick with me for treatment at my raptor center, Birds of Prey Northwest. After a week, I rode the bucket up again and returned the nestling to its home. Weeks later, nest cam viewers watched as the chick they helped rescue took its first flight.

Most entangled ospreys are never rescued, and entanglement is not just from fishing line. Plastic baling twine left on the ground, after livestock eat bales of hay, also ends up in nests. Ospreys are attracted to the twine's orange color, which looks like soft plants. When ospreys line their nests with twine, chicks or adults can get tangled.

As plastic pollution increases worldwide, new hazards end up in ospreys' habitat. Chicks are being rescued from plastic bags in their nests, that could smother them. Scientists worry that extremely tiny plastic pieces called microplastics, found in bodies of water and in fish, will harm ospreys by entering their food chain.

Over 20 years, environmental protection laws and osprey reintroduction in the U.S. made their species a wildlife conservation success. Protecting them now depends on all of us. Actions we take for the environment, like disposing of used fishing line and baling twine, reducing single use plastic bags, and protecting forest and marine ecosystems, will help ensure their survival. Ospreys are found on every continent except Antarctica, and migrate across countries and even between continents. This makes regional, national and international cooperation to protect them more important than ever.

All About Ospreys Species name *Pandion haliaetus*

What kinds of birds are ospreys?

Ospreys are birds of prey or raptors, like eagles, falcons, hawks and owls. Ospreys are their own species, found on every continent except Antarctica. They nest along shorelines of the ocean, bays, lakes, rivers, large ponds, and other bodies of water. In shallow waters they swoop and dive to catch fish, almost the only food they eat.

The father catches almost all the fish for young chicks to eat. The mother tears off pieces of fish to feed the chicks, until they are 4-5 weeks old and can do this

themselves. In open nests exposed to the Sun, mother ospreys have the critical job of shading chicks to keep them from overheating. Early in life, chicks can't control their body temperature to keep warm or cool.

Osprey chicks grow fast. By 6 weeks they're full size, with a typical wingspread of 5 feet (1.5 meters) for females and 4 feet (1.2 meters) for males, and stiff flight feathers covering their wings. Around 8-10 weeks nestlings take their first flights, called fledging. Fledglings need lots of practice to become skilled flyers and hunters. In flight, ospreys' wings clearly show an M shape—the top points are the wrist joints. Primary feathers from the wrists to the wingtips are the most important flight feathers.

Young ospreys become adults during their first, two-year-long migration. After that they migrate every year, often flying for days without resting. Bonded pairs mate for life but go on separate migrations, then return to meet again at their nest. When northern fishing waters freeze over, ospreys may migrate far across continents, and even to other continents where they can find food.

How do ospreys use their talons and beaks?

With long, curved talons, ospreys grab live fish, carry them in flight, and hold them while eating. Ospreys have four toes on each foot. Each toe has a talon that acts like a curved fishing hook. The bottoms of an osprey's feet and toes have sticky, spiked pads called spicules (a bit like sticky Velcro). Ospreys' powerful grasp, long talons, and sticky feet let them hold onto even the slipperiest fish.

When an osprey catches a fish, the talons lock in a tight grip. But the outer third toe on each foot is reversible. An osprey can flip that toe and its talon, so any fish it's carrying will point the same direction the osprey flies. This way the osprey meets less wind resistance and can fly faster, using less energy.

Like all birds of prey, ospreys slash with their talons to defend themselves and their young from predators. But when moving around in the nest, osprey parents curl their talons into a ball, so they won't hurt their chicks.

Ospreys use their beaks in different ways. They tear food from prey with their curved, sharp-tipped top beak, and scoop water with their lower beak. Using their whole beak, they preen their feathers, opening the tube-shaped quills so new feathers can unfurl, and smoothing older feathers into position. They waterproof their feathers by spreading oil from a special gland with their whole beak.

What other adaptations do ospreys have?

Adult ospreys weigh up to 4 pounds (1.8 kilograms) for females and 2 pounds (0.9 kilograms) for males. They're lightweight because their bones are hollow and they have air sacs throughout their body. When ospreys breathe, the air goes into their lungs, bones and air sacs.

Ospreys have spectacular adaptations for catching fish. Hovering about 30 feet (9 meters) above the water, they search for food in the shallows. Their eyes see about 10 times more detail over distance than a human's eyes can. Dark feathered stripes on an osprey's face help keep the Sun's glare out of the bird's eyes.

Ospreys swoop to catch fish from the surface, or dive almost straight down at 30 miles (48 kilometers) per hour. As they plunge, their eyes and wide-open talons face the "strike zone" where they will grab their prey. Ospreys crash into the water feet first and can go 3 feet (1 meter) underwater to grab fish. Their feet and stocky legs act like shock absorbers when they hit the water.

Underwater, ospreys can keep their eyes open. A see-through "third eyelid," called a nictitating membrane (like crocodiles have), protects their eyeballs. Meanwhile, the nostrils in an osprey's nose close underwater to keep water out. An osprey's chest muscles are so strong, when the bird dives below the surface, its wings can lift it out of the water and back into flight. If an osprey cannot lift itself, the bird uses its powerful wings like oars (as a bald eagle does) to row back to land.

Where do ospreys build their nests?

Where there are enough trees, ospreys build nests as high in trees as they can. They also nest on human-made structures like utility poles and bridges. In many areas with little natural nesting habitat, people set up platforms to give ospreys more sites for building nests.

Male ospreys choose where to build the nest, and carry large sticks and twigs in their talons. To line the nest, they bring grass, algae and other soft materials. Females shape and arrange the nest with their beaks. Over years, a pair may build their nest until it weighs 400 pounds (181 kilograms).

What happens when baby ospreys are lost from a nest?

Very young raptors are small and weak. Before they can fly, many are blown from nests during storms, jump from nests in extreme heat, or are bumped from nests by other chicks. Some get tangled in plastic that the father brings to the nest. Then the chicks can't move or fly, and even end up hanging from the nest, unable to get free.

The loss of all chicks from a nest triggers a change in osprey parents' brain chemicals, or hormones. This affects the parents' behavior—they no longer sense an attachment to the nest. The parents leave and don't return until the next year, or fly off and build a new nest somewhere else to hatch and raise new chicks.

How did ospreys become endangered? How did scientists save them from becoming extinct?

In 1976, ospreys were added to the U.S. Endangered Species List. Like bald eagles and peregrine falcons, they were endangered by human use of the insect-killing chemical DDT. In some states ospreys were nearly wiped out, and they even became extinct in certain areas.

When people sprayed DDT in the air to kill insects, the spray ended up on plants, crops and soils. Rain washed the DDT into bodies of water, where it got into eats a lead sinker attached to the line, the bird develops deadly lead poisoning.

Where livestock are fed bales of hay outdoors, ospreys may pick up soft plastic baling twine left on the ground. Carried into the nest, the twine entangles and injures ospreys so they can't move or fly. Plastic

bags or packaging, that can smother a chick, may be carried into a nest by osprey parents or blown there by the wind. Microplastics, extremely tiny plastic bits, in water can enter ospreys' bodies when they drink, or when they eat fish with microplastics in their bodies.

Building homes, hotels, and businesses along shorelines destroys osprey habitat. Habitat destruction forces ospreys to nest farther from water. Since osprey parents must bring fresh fish to their chicks every few hours, nesting far from water puts tremendous strain on parents feeding their young.

Swoop and Soar and *Beauty and the Beak*, both coauthored by Deborah Lee Rose and raptor biologist Janie Veltkamp, are true stories of how Janie rescues real birds of prey and uses STEM to help them survive. In *Swoop and Soar*, Janie helps two orphan osprey chicks go back into the wild. In *Beauty and the Beak*, a bald eagle gets a new 3D-printed, prosthetic beak but must remain in Janie's care.

SWOOP AND SOAR

HOW SCIENCE RESCUED TWO OSPREY ORPHANS AND FOUND THEM A NEW FAMILY IN THE WILD

By Deborah Lee Rose and Jane Veltkamp

- After you read both books, why do you think there is such a big difference in the stories' endings?

- What do the photos in the books show you about how the two stories are different, but in some ways alike?

- Can you find a scene and photo in *Swoop and Soar* that directly connects ospreys and bald eagles?

In the two true stories, Janie needs to know a lot about raptors and their adaptations for survival.

- How are ospreys and bald eagles the same, like in where they live, or their adaptations including beaks and talons?

- How are ospreys and bald eagles different, like in how they fly and hunt for food?

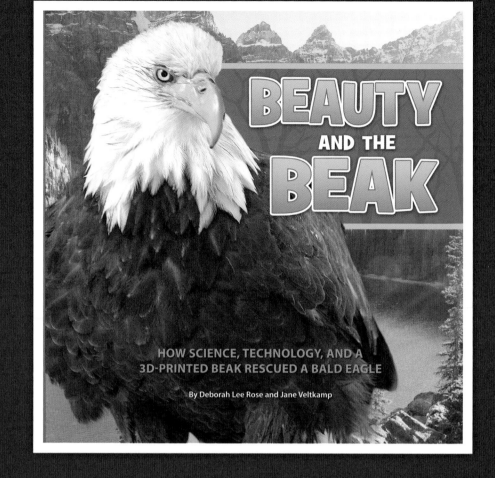

BEAUTY AND THE BEAK

HOW SCIENCE, TECHNOLOGY, AND A 3D-PRINTED BEAK RESCUED A BALD EAGLE

By Deborah Lee Rose and Jane Veltkamp

In **Swoop and Soar**, the osprey orphans need a new nest and parents. In **Beauty and the Beak**, the bald eagle needs a new beak. Janie has to figure out how she can use STEM to help these two kinds of raptors with very different needs.

- How does Janie use the process of observation to help the ospreys and the bald eagle in different ways?

- Why does Janie have to act quickly to help the ospreys find a new nest, but needs a lot more time to engineer a 3D-printed, prosthetic beak for Beauty?

When Ospreys Need Care

If you see an osprey or other raptor on the ground or hanging from a nest—or if you're watching a nest cam and something looks wrong—quickly contact a raptor or wildlife organization, center or agency, a local veterinarian, or the organization that operates the nest cam. Rapid care increases the bird's chance of surviving.

How You Can Help Ospreys

- You can support organizations that rescue ospreys, protect their nests and habitat, or build platforms for them to nest on. You may able to volunteer to help ospreys too.

- You can ask your school or community group to invite a raptor educator to speak in person or virtually. Have the educator include a live osprey or other raptor if possible.

- You can join a coastal or watershed cleanup with your family, school, scout troop, community group, or faith organization, or a wildlife or environmental nonprofit.

- You can use your words and actions. Let your elected representatives and town or city staff know you support efforts to protect ospreys and other wildlife.

What You Can Do to Learn More

Find out where you can go to see live ospreys in the wild, from resources like a state wildlife department or raptor education center. Another great way to observe wild ospreys in their high nests is by watching an osprey nest cam. Such cameras are located across the U.S. and in some other countries, and their video is livestreamed and archived online. We recommmend checking out webcams that share some osprey nests you can visit virtually (whether ospreys are in the nest depends on the season and other factors). Here are a few to get you started...

WEBCAMS!

WATCH LIVE OSPREYS ON THESE WEBCAMS!

- **The Cornell Lab of Ornithology Savannah Ospreys Cam** in Georgia at https://www.allaboutbirds.org/cams/savannah-ospreys/, and **Hellgate Ospreys Nest Cam** in Montana at https://www.allaboutbirds.org/cams/hellgate-ospreys/

- **Sandpoint Osprey Cam** in Idaho at https://ospreys.sandpointonline.com

- **Barnegat Light Osprey Cam** in New Jersey (Conserve Wildlife Foundation of New Jersey) at http://www.conservewildlifenj.org/education/ospreycam/

Resources

Birds of Prey Northwest
Northern Idaho / Janie Veltkamp, Founding Director / BirdsOfPreyNorthwest.org
BOPNW is the nonprofit raptor education and rehabilitation center where Janie Veltkamp rescues ospreys, and where thousands of raptors have been given medical treatment with the purpose of returning them to the wild. In person in the U.S. Pacific Northwest, and virtually throughout the U.S., Janie Veltkamp educates people of all ages through programs involving specially trained educational birds of prey.

- Educational guide to *Swoop and Soar*
- Live raptor programs, and author visits including *Swoop and Soar* and *Beauty and the Beak: How Science, Technology, and a 3D-Printed Beak Rescued a Bald Eagle*

The Cornell Lab of Ornithology, Cornell University
https://www.allaboutbirds.org/guide/Osprey/id

USFWS National Wildlife Refuge System
https://www.fws.gov/refuge/McNary/Wildlife_Habitat/Ospreys.html

STEM Vocabulary

adaptations

algae

baling twine

binoculars

bioindicator

biologist

bird of prey

bonded

camouflage

chemical

climate change

conservation

cross fostering

DDT

ecosystem

electrocuted

endangered

energy

entanglement

environmental

extinct

fledging

food chain

force

forest canopy

forest floor

gland

habitat

hack box

hazards

hormones

imprint

incubator

leg band

magnifying scope

marine

microplastics

migration

molt

nest cam

nesting platform

nictitating membrane

nostrils

observation

pollution

population

predator

preen

prey

quills

raptor

reintroduction

risk

scientists

species

spicules

talons

wildlife

wind resistance

wingspread

Acknowledgments

Nature World Wildlife Rescue Sanctuary, Homosassa, Florida; Conserve Wildlife Foundation of New Jersey; Catherine Halversen; and Sandy and Doug Lindhout The two osprey chicks were rescued in Cedar Key, Florida. Janie heard about their plight as a member of the Cedar Key Audubon chapter.

Photo Credits

Front Cover: © Ann Kamzelski

Back Cover: © Ben Wurst

Larry Krumpelman © Jane Veltkamp

Ken Rohling © Jane Veltkamp

Back jacket flap: Jane Veltkamp photo by

Glen Hush © Jane Veltkamp

4 Shutterstock.com

5 © Michele Barker, photographer

6 © Michele Barker, photographer

7 © Scalder Photography

8 © Ben Wurst

9 © Cornell University

10 Marshalgonz / Shutterstock.com

11 PQN Studios / Shutterstock.com

12 Steve Bower / Shutterstock.com

15 Frank Morgan © Jane Veltkamp

17 Rob Rugur © Jane Veltkamp

20 Frank Morgan © Jane Veltkamp

21 Ken Rohling ©Jane Veltkamp

22 Paul Vinten / Shutterstock.com

23 Ken Rohling © Jane Veltkamp

24 Ken Rohling © Jane Veltkamp

26-27 Larry Krumpelman © Jane Vetlkamp

28 Larry Krumpelman © Jane Veltkamp

29 Ken Rohling © Jane Veltkamp

30-31 Frank Morgan © Jane Veltkamp

32 Frank Morgan © Jane Veltkamp

33 Mary Gertsema © Jane Veltkamp

35 Kjell Schioberg © Jane Veltkamp

37 Wirestock Creators / Shutterstock.com

38 USGS by John J. Mosesso

40 Larry Krumpelman © Jane Veltkamp

41 U.S. National Park Service

43 © Ben Wurst

45 Ken Rohling © Jane Veltkamp

47 Kjell Schioberg © Jane Veltkamp

48 Jill Hamm © Jane Veltkamp

49 © Ben Wurst

50 Swoop and Soar cover © Ann Kamzelski

51 Beauty and the Beak cover Glen Hush © Jane Veltkamp

56 Jane Veltkamp photo Glen Hush © Jane Veltkamp

Osprey webcam photo (9) permission granted by Skidaway Audubon, aligned with their educational and conservation mission.

About the Authors

DEBORAH LEE ROSE coauthored the children's book *Beauty and the Beak: How Science, Technology, and a 3D-Printed Beak Rescued a Bald Eagle*, winner of the AAAS/Subaru SB&F Prize for Excellence in Science Books, the Bank Street College Cook Prize for Best STEM Picture Book, and the California Reading Association Eureka! Gold Award for Nonfiction. Deborah is the author of bestselling and beloved books read around the world, including *Astronauts Zoom! An Astronaut Alphabet* about the International Space Station, *Scientists Get Dressed, Jimmy the Joey, The Twelve Days of Winter*, and *Ocean Babies*. She speaks to schools and libraries, professional conferences and organizations. After many years in Northern California, Deborah now lives in Silver Spring, MD. Visit her website at ***deborahleerose.com***.

JANE VELTKAMP coauthored the children's book *Beauty and the Beak: How Science, Technology, and a 3D-Printed Beak Rescued a Bald Eagle*, winner of the AAAS/Subaru SB&F Prize for Excellence in Science Books, the Bank Street College Cook Prize for Best STEM Picture Book, and the California Reading Association Eureka! Gold Award for Nonfiction. A raptor biologist and educator, Jane is founding director of the nonprofit Birds of Prey Northwest in northern Idaho. She cares for Beauty the bald eagle, ospreys and raptors of all kinds, and leads raptor education programs involving live, specially trained educational birds. She directed the successful reintroduction of ospreys in eastern South Dakota. She rescues and treats wild raptors under permit from the U.S. Fish and Wildlife Service. She is the osprey expert for the Sandpoint, Idaho osprey nest cam. Visit her website at ***birdsofpreynorthwest.org***.